MONSTER LUNCH

PAT SKENE

Illustrated by Graham Ross

ORCA BOOK PUBLISHERS

*For the whole gang: Zach, Evan, Farrell, Kiya, Sabey,
Joshua, Jake and Jaimy—Happy Reading!*

Author Note: Many thanks to the website **www.soupsong.com**
for permission to use some of the jokes posted on their site.

Text copyright © 2008 Pat Skene
Illustrations copyright © 2008 Graham Ross

Library and Archives Canada Cataloguing in Publication

Skene, Pat, 1945-
Monster lunch / written by Pat Skene ; illustrator, Graham Ross.

(Orca echoes)
ISBN 978-1-55143-941-9

1. Food--Juvenile fiction. 2. Children's stories, Canadian (English).
3. Stories in rhyme. 4. Food--Miscellanea--Juvenile literature.
I. Ross, Graham, 1962- II. Title. III. Series.

PS8637.K46M65 2008   jC813'.6   C2008-903427-9

First published in the United States, 2008
Library of Congress Control Number: 2008930034

Summary: Yummy, yucky, messy and hot rhyming stories and fascinating facts about food.

Orca Book Publishers gratefully acknowledges the support for its publishing programs provided by the
following agencies: the Government of Canada through the Book Publishing Industry Development
Program and the Canada Council for the Arts, and the Province of British Columbia through the
BC Arts Council and the Book Publishing Tax Credit.

Typesetting by Teresa Bubela
Cover artwork and interior illustrations by Graham Ross
Author photo by Cindy Taylor

ORCA BOOK PUBLISHERS
PO Box 5626, STN. B
VICTORIA, BC CANADA
V8R 6S4

ORCA BOOK PUBLISHERS
PO Box 468
CUSTER, WA USA
98240-0468

www.orcabook.com
Printed and bound in Canada.

011 010 09 08   •   4 3 2 1

Contents

Monster Lunch

I plan to dine with Frankenstein,
  and you're invited too!
Please bring your monster appetite,
  you might try something new.

For lunch we're having spinach puffs,
  lobster claws and clams.
Hot gooey cheese on broccoli,
  with sweet brown-sugared yams.

You'll love my leeks and lima beans,
  cold liverwurst with prunes.
And monster scoops of whipping cream,
  on chocolate macaroons.

I'll chill a pail of ginger ale,
  so we can sip a drink.
We'll snack on roasted garlic buds,
  and make a monster-stink.

Then if we have an appetite,
   for gumbo or ragout,
I'll make a chunky oxtail soup
   and rutabaga stew.

This hungry monster-friend of mine
   would never hurt a fly.
But here's a treat he's sure to eat—
   my yummy shoofly pie.

Now Frankenstein might goof around
   and stick food up his nose.
He could be wearing monster boots,
   so please protect your toes!

If he should dance, we'll have a chance
   to watch the monster-mash.
He'll romp and stomp his monster lunch
   into a monster hash.

And when he eats, he'll *SLOSH* and *SLURP*,
  and *CRUNCH* and *CRUNCH* and *CRUNCH*!
Big monsters make a monster-mess,
  when monsters come for lunch.

Oh yes, and here's another thing—
  at times he can be rude.
He'll make those belly-belching *BURPS,*
  'cause he's that kind of dude.

So please drop by—he's quite a guy
  and funnier than heck.
You've got to see him swallow
  with that bolt stuck through his neck.

He's sure to be the perfect guest,
  for any feast of mine.
RSVP—I hope you're free
  to dine with Frankenstein!

The Eater's Digest

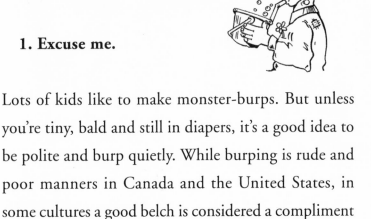

1. Excuse me.

Lots of kids like to make monster-burps. But unless you're tiny, bald and still in diapers, it's a good idea to be polite and burp quietly. While burping is rude and poor manners in Canada and the United States, in some cultures a good belch is considered a compliment to the cook. There are even birds that burp to attract a mate. It sure doesn't work that way with people!

2. No flies in my pies.

If you like sweets, you'll love shoofly pie. It's like coffee cake with a gooey molasses bottom. (Molasses is thick syrup made from sugarcane.) These pies got their weird name years ago, when the sweet ingredients attracted flies and cooks had to "shoo" the flies away. Try it! It's delicious with whipped cream or chocolate icing.

3. Monster breath.

Garlic has been around for over six thousand years! In ancient times, the Egyptians built the pyramids on a simple diet of dates, garlic, bread and water. Not only does garlic spice up dinner, but it's been known to cure and prevent a lot of diseases. Some people rub garlic on the soles of their feet to cure a cold. Imagine that! Get rid of a runny nose with stinky toes.

4. Soup tales.

Shoofly pie may not have any flies, but oxtail soup really *does* have oxtails in it. This soup is made from the skinned tail of an ox. It's like beef soup with vegetables and spices. The oxtail is cut into small chunks, so don't worry, you won't see a tail hanging out of the pot. Go ahead and try some—if you're monster-brave enough.

7

5. How sweet it is.

Sugar is so yummy, especially in desserts. But sugar is sneaky and hides in other stuff like ketchup, bread, pasta and even in cough medicine. There are seven teaspoons of sugar in one can of cola. So watch your sweet-o-meter. Too much sugar can rot your teeth and make you sick. Here's one good way to tame your sugar-monster: Eat broccoli!

6. Manners matter.

Did you know that RSVP stands for the French phrase "Répondez s'il vous plaît," which means "Please reply"? So if you get an invitation with the letters *RSVP* written on it, make sure you RSVP—ASAP!

Archibald Burkle's Burgoo

Excitement in Muddville had started at dawn.
The day of the town picnic was here.
Mayor Archibald Burkle was sure his burgoo
would become the event of the year.

The tiny round mayor picked his favorite bow tie.
Then he straightened his jacket once more.
"This day will be perfect," he said in the mirror.
But he didn't know what was in store.

Kids ran to the park where balloons filled the air,
and the crowd cheered, "Hip-hip-hooray!"
The mayor had declared no expense would be spared,
so he hired the Mudds for the day.

In Muddville, the Mudds band was known far and wide.
They played country bluegrass and rock.
The townspeople crowded in front of the stage.
And the mayor picked the mike up to talk.

"As Muddville's burgoo-meister," Archibald said,
"I declare this will be quite a do!
The weather looks fine, so I guess it's a sign.
Now nothing can stop our burgoo!"

The picnic got started and tables were set.
Mrs. Roy put out salads and rolls.
Bob's Curly-Q Chip Truck was sizzling with fries.
There were barbecued ribs on the coals.

Three big iron kettles were filled with burgoo,
and volunteers stirred them with care.
The long wooden paddles they used for the stew
had been chosen this year by the mayor.

When suddenly there was a big gust of wind,
swirling dirt-devils twirled in the sand.
The wind grew and blew, dumping tables of food,
and paper plates flew at the band.

Salads lay scattered all over the ground.
The ribs were now covered in dirt.
A roll hit the mayor in the head, and he said,
"I'm okay, folks, I haven't been hurt!"

Mayor Archibald Burkle's burgoo was a mess.
And the whirlwind destroyed the buffet.
He said, "Good Muddvillers, our picnic is ruined.
I'm so sorry, the wind spoiled our day."

Then all of the children called out to the mayor,
"But we've still got our three pots of stew."
"We can't let a little wind mess up our fun."
"You said nothing could stop our burgoo!"

And just at that moment, thunder clouds *CRACKED*.
"Oh no!" cried the mayor to the group.
Rain filled the kettles and thinned the burgoo.
Now the stew looked like watery soup.

The soggy Mudds scrambled to get their guitars,
when the wind and rain finally stopped.
Soaking-wet banners had blown on the stage,
and the picnic balloons were all popped.

Mayor Burkle's toupee slipped over his eyes.
"I declare!" he said, blushing bright red.
He slipped off the wig and gave it a shake,
then stuck it right back on his head.

Burgoo-meister Burkle announced once again,
"I declare, as the mayor of this town,
our picnic is ruined—it's over and done.
The burgoo is just too watered down."

"Let's get more potatoes!" cried Timmy O'Toole.
"We'll throw them all into the stew."
"More beans," said Matilda. "Come on everyone.
Nothing can stop our burgoo!"

The Muddvillers joined in the chopping and peeling.
It wasn't a difficult chore.
The rainwater thinned out the three pots of stew,
so they thickened it up to make more.

The mayor was perplexed and thought,
"What could be next?" Poor Archy began to perspire.
All sweaty, he twitched as his wet toupee itched.
Then Curly-Q-Bob hollered, "FIRE!"

The chip truck was smoking and pumping out soot.
In a flash, the crowd started to shout.
People grabbed buckets filled up by the rain
and then worked till the fire went out.

Burgoo-meister Burkle sat down with a *PLOP*!
He was glad all the folks were okay.
With dirt on his shirt, he said, "No one's been hurt.
I declare! We should call it a day."

The mayor shook his head, and he sighed as he said,
"What a terrible hullabaloo."
But then the kids cried, "We declare Mr. Mayor,
you said nothing could stop our burgoo!"

The Muddvillers shrugged, and then everyone hugged,
leaving Archibald rather confused.
The Mudds played so loud that old Grandma McLeod,
tapped her toe to the beat while she snoozed.

The kids held their races with turtles and frogs.
And burgoo-goers gathered to talk.
Archy took off his wig and hoe-downed a jig.
Now the Mudds really started to rock.

They cranked up the amps for their twangy guitars.
What a toe-tapping beat! What a crowd!
Folks lined up for so many bowls of burgoo,
that it made the burgoo-meister proud.

That evening when all the festivities stopped,
and the mayor helped the cleaning-up crew,
"I declare!" he recalled. "We got through it all.
Nothing could stop our burgoo!"

An Interview with Mayor Archibald Burkle

1. Is "burgoo" a real word?

Archibald Burkle: I declare, it certainly is, and it has two meanings. A burgoo can be a thick, spicy delicious stew. It can also be a picnic or an outdoor festival where burgoo stew is served—hopefully on a nice day. But then again, rain or shine, nothing can stop a good burgoo, I always say.

2. What was in your burgoo stew?

Archibald Burkle: In the pioneer days, they made burgoo stew with squirrel meat. But today, most people use chicken, beef, pork or lamb instead. We used a variety of different meats, including a few well-seasoned ham knuckles. Then we added tons of fresh vegetables, beans and lots of spices. It was burgoo-licious!

3. How do you cook it?

Archibald Burkle: We had lots of people to feed, so we cooked it outside in huge iron kettles. Our burgoo pots were as big around as hula hoops. Volunteers took turns stirring the burgoo with long wooden paddles, over an open wood fire. They started the day before the picnic and stirred the pots all night. The burgoo stirrers sure were tired in the morning. But they stayed awake for the picnic and ate lots of bowls of burgoo.

4. What's a "burgoo-meister"?

Archibald Burkle: It's pronounced "ber-goo-my-ster." This title is a special honor given to the person who gets to decide what will go into the burgoo stew. I declared myself the burgoo-meister for my own picnic. That way, I could add my special blend of spices. It was my great granny's secret burgoo recipe. I come from a long line of budding Burkle burgoo-meisters.

5. What else did you eat at your burgoo?

Archibald Burkle: Well, lots of picnic food was ruined in the wind and rain. But I did get to eat some of Bob's delicious curly fries. That is, before his chip truck caught fire. Cooking French fries can be dangerous. Bob foolishly left the chips sizzling on the stove and went outside to listen to the Mudds. That's when the hot oil burst into flames. Luckily no one was hurt. I declare! He won't do that again!

Rhyme Time News

Little Boy Blue, come blow your horn.
Read *Rhyme Time*'s breaking news!
Old Mother Goose's nursery rhymes
have changed with modern views.

> Would you agree?
> Read on and see.

When poor Jack Sprat could eat no fat,
his wife asked for his share.
She ate the fat, left there by Jack,
and broke the kitchen chair.

> Too much fat.
> What good is that?

Miss Muffet ate her curds and whey,
then couldn't stand the shame.
When all that lactose gave her gas,
the spider got the blame.

> She bloated up,
>
> on just one cup.

When Old King Cole called for his bowl,
he ate and ate and ate.
That merry man loved fast-food junk,
and royally gained weight.

> All snacks and fries,
>
> not very wise.

The Queen of Hearts made butter tarts.
The knave stole them away.
"You're diabetic!" cried the king,
and took them back that day.
> The king forgave
> that reckless knave.

Mary, Mary felt contrary.
Pollen made her cranky.
So when her garden grew, she blew
and honked into her hanky.
> How Mary wheezed.
> She sneezed and sneezed.

Jack was nimble, Jack was quick.
That boy was not a klutz.
He'd jump clear over candlesticks
to get away from nuts!
> The kid was slick.
> Nuts made him sick.

Little Bo Peep lost all her sheep
and didn't want to find them.
She got a prickly rash from wool
and itched too much to mind them.
    She scratched and scratched
    till they dispatched.

So, Polly put the kettle on.
Let's drink organic tea.
Read *Rhyme Time News* for changing views
on how things used to be.
    Some silly rhymes,
    for modern times.

Jack & Jill's Report from the Hill

1. The skinny on fats.

We all need fat in our diets. Good fat—from food like fish—helps kids develop healthy thinking brains. But eating too much fat like Mrs. Sprat (especially bad fats), can make us unhealthy. Most fruits and vegetables have almost no fat at all. The real nasty fats are lurking in fast foods, packaged snacks, desserts and fried foods. So be wise—watch your pies and fries!

2. Slow down on fast food.

You're smart enough to know that junk food is not really made from garbage. But fast-food junk is chock-a-block full of salt, sugar and gobs of bad fat. Eating junk food once in a while is okay. But don't be like King Cole. Stay on junk patrol. Leave some room in your bowl for good food everyday.

3. What are "curds and whey"?

As you know, cheese is made from milk. During the cheese-making process and before the cheese is ready, lumpy bits called "curds" are formed. The curds are slippery and squishy. They float around in cloudy yellowish water called "whey." The whey tastes just like milk. Now if you're also wondering about Miss Muffet's "tuffet"—it was probably a stool.

4. What a gas!

How would you like to feel bloated and gassy after eating yummy cheese pizza and ice cream? That's what it feels like to be lactose intolerant. Lactose is a type of sugar found in milk and dairy foods. Lots of people have trouble digesting food with lactose. It's not serious. You just have to watch what you eat. Poor Miss Muffet had a lactose problem after eating her milky snack. Phew!

5. When good sugar goes bad.

Our body needs sugar for energy. But for kids with diabetes the body can't process sugar properly.

Too much sugar stays in their blood and makes them sick. They often take medicine that helps the body process sugar in the right way. Kids who are diabetic, like the knave, can't eat a lot of sweets. But they need to eat often, and exercise is important too. So maybe that reckless knave should have been playing soccer instead of stealing tarts.

6. Achooooooo!

Lots of kids have allergies. Some kids sneeze and have itchy watery eyes when there's too much pollen in the air. Others might get a rash like Bo Peep when they're around furry animals. Dust mites and mold can trigger allergy problems too. Many kids have bad reactions to certain foods, especially nuts. Sometimes allergies might even make you feel contrary, just like Mary. If that happens to you—try writing a silly rhyme to cheer yourself up. Mother Goose won't mind!

Hot Zoop!

My name is Soozy Quackenbush.
    They call me Soozy Q.
I've got the strangest tale to tell.
    You won't believe it's true.

The whole thing started in my bowl,
    when I sat down to lunch.
I love zoo crackers in my soup,
    so I threw in a bunch.

They floated in my noodle soup.
　　　My bowl looked like a zoo.
And then I heard them calling me,
　　　"Hey, you there, Soozy Q.!"

Now, when I blew the steam away,
　　　they cried, "Don't eat us yet."
Then one of those zoo crackers yelled,
　　　"Look out or you'll get wet!"

What I saw next was rather strange.
　　　Those crackers all jumped out.
I watched them stampede from my bowl.
　　　"Hot zoop!" I heard them shout.

Then all these little animals
　　　grew big and tall like me.
They said, "We're glad to meet you kid,"
　　　and shook my hand with glee.

Some names were odd, like Moo-Moo Maude,
and Buck from Timbuktu.
And Franny Frog from Foggy Bog,
and Kit from Katmandu.

They leaped around the kitchen floor
and made a soupy mess.
I giggled when that Moo-Moo cow,
put on my Aunt Bea's dress.

Then Dancing Dan Orangutan
stomped out a monkey beat.
He sure was one cool cracker-dude
with funky monkey feet.

A parakeet named Sneaky Pete
peeked inside my pocket.
I said, "Hey, you! Get out of there.
Give me back my locket."

Now, Bo Regard, the Saint Bernard,
    tried out my hula hoop.
But Bo got so dog-tired out,
    his jowls drooped in my soup.

And in a while, the crocodile
    said, "Howdy, Soozy Q."
He ate my dirty sneakers, burped
    and said, "I'm Croc McDoo."

Then Buck the camel joined the fun
    and bumped me off my chair.
He grinned a bit, and then he spit.
    He camel-juiced my hair!

"Behave yourselves," I told them all.
    "And get back in my bowl.
You're not where you're supposed to be.
    You're all out of control!"

"The zoop's too hot," meowed Kit the cat.
       "We can't go back in yet.
The steam will burn our noses and…
       hot noodles make us sweat."

"We'd like to stick around," cried Buck.
       "We'll dance and sing a song.
And then we'll spit—I mean we'll split.
       We won't stay very long."

They pleaded, "Pleeeeeeeeze! Miss Soozy Q.
       Come on…what do you say?"
Their soupy faces nuzzled me,
       until I said, "Okay…"

"Yippee," they hollered one by one.
       "It's time to rock and roll."
"Have fun," I said, "but don't forget—
       you're going back in that bowl."

Now Moo-Moo Maude liked fifties tunes.
  She mooed *My Moo-Suede Shoes*.
When Franny croaked, *Down on the Bog*,
  Bo howled those doggone blues.

Old Croc McDoo crooned country songs,
  while Buck bucked to the beat.
Cool Dancing Dan Orangutan
  rapped hip-hop rhymes with Pete.

"I think you're flat," yowled Kit the cat.
  But they could not care less.
I hoped Aunt Bea would never see,
  that Moo-cow in her dress.

"All you animals are crackers,"
  I told them with a grin.
And sure enough, when my soup cooled,
  they waved and jumped back in.

They called out, "Bye, Miss Soozy Q.
We liked you quite a lot.
But when you put us in your zoop,
make sure it's not too hot!"

An Interview with Soozy Q. about Soup

1. What kind of soup were you eating?

Soozy Q.: I was having steamy, hot, chicken noodle soup. I really like to slurp the noodles. But most people say that soup should be seen and not heard. Some soups have funny names like: mulligatawny, gazpacho, cocky-leeky and knickerbocker. There's even a mock turtle soup that doesn't have any turtles in it. I know lots of things about soup. And I know a lot of soup jokes too.

Question: What do you call a chicken in a hot tub?
Answer: Soup!

2. Do you know where soup comes from?

Soozy Q.: Soup started out as a gruel or porridge. Then when bread was invented, people poured liquids over a piece of bread in a bowl. They called it "sop" or "sup." Over time, this became the "soup" we know today. Maybe that's where "supper" came from too. And now we have soup for supper.

Question: What is Dracula's favorite soup?
Answer: Scream of tomato.

3. When did people start making soup?

Soozy Q.: Soup has been around for thousands of years. Every culture in the world has a history of making soup. In the early days, soup spoons were made from wood and animal horns. But before spoons were invented, people drank the soup right from the bowl. They just picked out the chunky bits with their fingers. I guess it was finger-licking-good soup!

Question: When is rabbit soup not so good?
Answer: When there's a hare in it.

4. What's your favorite soup?

Soozy Q.: I haven't got a favorite. I like them all. There are so many different kinds. There are thin soups, thick soups, smooth soups, cold soups, chunky soups and even dried soups. Soup lore has it that a thin clear broth called consommé was created for a French king. He wanted to see his reflection in the bowl.

Question: How do you make gold soup?
Answer: With twenty-two carrots.

5. Do you still put animal crackers in your soup?

Soozy Q.: I sure do—they're the best! Did you know that animal crackers have been around for over one hundred years? But they started out as biscuits and cookies shaped like animals. A long time ago, they were also called "circus crackers." And in 1902, you could even buy animal crackers in a box that looked like a circus wagon. They sold for five cents a box. What a deal!

Question: What do ducks have for lunch?
Answer: Soup and quackers.

6. What are dried soups?

Soozy Q.: The ingredients for these soups are freeze-dried and put into packages. Dried soups are

39

quick and easy to make and can be eaten anywhere. You just add water to them. They're great for hiking and camping trips. Mountain climbers put dried soups in their backpacks. Then all they have to do is melt snow to make hot soup on a cold mountain. Cool!

Question: What does a dragon eat with soup?
Answer: Firecrackers.

Grumpy Garden-Dude

Please excuse my attitude,
but you can keep your garden-food.
I think planting is a bore,
when you can buy stuff at the store.

One day my dad said with a grin,
"C'mon, let's put a garden in."
I dragged the tools down from the shelf
and kept my feelings to myself.

We found a sunny garden spot.
I worked till I was sweaty hot.
We turned the soil to make a bed.
"Now add manure," my father said.

"Phew!" I cried. "Give me a break!"
He laughed and handed me the rake.
I sniffed and sniffed but must admit,
it didn't even stink a bit.

We put in rows and rows of seeds.
Dad said, "That's what our garden needs."
We planted seedlings in the ground
and wrapped some wire all around.

I moaned and groaned till we were done.
My dad said, "Next comes all the fun.
I'll make a gardener of you yet."
I answered, "Right! You wanna bet?"

I dug my heels into the dirt
and wiped my hands across my shirt.
Now what's a grumpy dude to do?
I didn't have a garden-clue!

For weeks I battled wicked weeds.
I shrieked at slugs and centipedes.
The sprinkler hose had sprung a leak.
My garden-life was looking bleak.

Then day by day, the changes came.
And things no longer looked the same.
Who knew that peas could climb a pole?
Or squash would grow out of control?

We built a trellis with some twine.
I helped my dad with the design.
We scooped up radishes and beans,
picked carrots, beets and lettuce greens.

Our yard looked like a grocery mart.
I could have used a shopping cart.
Tomatoes overflowed my pot,
and suddenly, I had a thought.

"It's pizza night," I told my dad.
I showed him all the stuff I had.
Red peppers, onions, herbs and more.
"We don't need pizza from the store."

We made the dough—it was a breeze.
I cooked the sauce and added cheese.
I gave the first slice to my dad.
It was the best he ever had!

So now this grumpy garden-dude,
is really into growing food.
I grew a cuke—big as a log!
I grew a gourd—shaped like a hog!

I tried to plant a pizza crust,
but all I got was dirt and dust.
Now just how tricky could it be
to grow a pepperoni tree?

Digging up the Facts

1. The radish wins.

Many gardeners say that radishes are the fastest growing vegetable. Most veggies grow in about forty-five days. But radishes can go from seed to your lunch box in under one month. Most radishes are crunchy and hot. Radish juice is supposed to be good for sore throats and colds. So next time you have the sniffles, try squeezing a radish.

2. The eyes have it.

The only way to grow a potato is to plant a potato. You need a potato with "eyes" on the skin. These eyes are potato buds, and they grow new potatoes when you plant them. Just cut a potato into four pieces.

Then put the pieces in the ground with the eyes pointing up. Soon you'll be digging up one potato, two potato, three potato, four...and maybe more.

3. The lady and the toad.

There are lots of bugs and critters lining up to chomp away on your garden goodies. But not all of them want to eat your vegetables. Ladybugs and toads actually help your garden. They eat the pesky bugs that like to feast on your veggie plants. So give these two friendly helpers a big lunchtime welcome.

4. Grub in a tub.

If you don't have a spot for a garden plot, use a pot. Almost anything can be used as a container. Look around for cans, boots, barrels and maybe even an old bathtub. You'll need an adult to help you fill the containers with soil and get them ready for planting.

Cherry tomatoes, strawberries and peas would make delicious snacks-in-a-pot, don't you think?

5. More food for thought.

Garden lore has it that a herb called basil will keep witches away—even on Halloween. And did you know that both vampires and mosquitoes don't like garlic? Come to think of it...vampires and mosquitoes have a lot in common, don't they? So remember: Eat garlic tonight, the stinky delight. And smell as you might, you won't get a bite!

My Birthday Mess
—by Tess

My birthday started in a mess,
when Mom said, "Go get ready, Tess."
She made me wear a stupid dress
and wash my stupid hair.

At three o'clock, I kicked a chair.
No kids had come, it wasn't fair!
Balloons were hanging everywhere.
I paced around the room.

The house was quiet as a tomb.
My birthday-temper made me fume.
I wallowed in my doom and gloom
and forced myself to sit.

49

But waiting didn't help a bit.
I felt so angry, I could spit.
I worked myself into a snit
and tried hard not to bawl.

My birthday cake was in the hall.
I grabbed it—candles, plate and all—
and smashed it up against the wall.
My mother cried, "Dear me!"

Before I got the third degree,
I hollered, "So? Where can they be?
My friends should have been here by three!"
I was seeing red.

Mom saw the cake and shook her head.
"Oh, Tess…" was all my mother said.
"Your birthday invitation read,
The party starts at four."

Just then my guests came in the door
with birthday gifts and smiles galore.
They saw my cake-mess on the floor
and did a double-take.

I mumbled, "Er…a big mistake.
I kind of…sort of…dropped my cake.
But maybe…you could help me bake."
They cheered, "Hip-hip-hooray!"

Before my mom knew what to say,
the party gang sang, "Cakes-away!
We're here to bake a cake today!"
I laughed and cried, "Encore!"

We opened up the cupboard door
and found what we were looking for.
But we forgot our baking chore
and had a flour fight.

Our kitchen walls were dusted white.
It made a spooky birthday sight.
We partied up an appetite
and ate an ice-cream roll.

Our cake brigade marched on patrol.
We drummed a metal mixing bowl.
My party guests had lost control,
but then we stopped to bake.

They wanted separate cakes to make,
so each could decorate a cake.
I screamed, "Give me a stupid break!"
and called them something rude.

My temper ruined the party mood.
I looked out at my party brood.
No birthday cake, no party food.
No "Happy Birthday, Tess."

53

I stood there in my party dress,
and knew I'd made another mess.
I said, "I guess I must confess,
I'm such a drama queen."

I blurted out, "I didn't mean,
to call you names or make a scene.
I know how horrible I've been."
I tried hard not to cry.

And then I looked them in the eye
and asked them not to say good-bye.
I promised them I'd really try.
My chin began to shake.

I knew how long that it would take
to make each one of them a cake.
But smaller cakes were quick to bake.
I said, "I have a plan."

"Let's stir the batter," I began.
"And bake it in a muffin pan.
I make this recipe with Gran.
We like it quite a bit."

My cupcakes were the biggest hit.
I said, "I'm glad we didn't quit.
I'm sorry for my hissy fit.
Who wants the sprinkle-pops?"

We decorated all the tops,
with frosting and some lollypops.
We added sour cherry-drops,
and chunks of chocolate too.

Now when my birthday bash was through,
I wrote this poem to share with you.
And in the end, I think I grew.
Those cupcakes were the best!

An Interview with Tess about Cake

1. What's your favorite cake?

Tess: This is embarrassing. But the cake I smashed against the wall was my favorite. And it was called a Smash Cake even before I smashed it. Helping Mom make this kind of cake is always the best part. I get to smash a bag of cookies and add the broken chunks to the batter. I guess that's why it's called Smash Cake. Too bad I lost my temper and *really* smashed my Smash Cake.

2. Do you like making cakes?

Tess: I sure do! I might even be a baker someday. That way, I could create my own super-yummy cakes.

Some cakes have cool names, like Hummingbird Cake, Angel Food Cake, Devil's Food Cake and 1234 Cake. Maybe I could invent a Birthday-Mess Cake.

3. Where did you learn to make cupcakes?

Tess: I didn't know how to make them—it just worked out. Last year, my Gran taught me to make an old-fashioned 1234 Cake. It's easy to remember: one cup of butter, two cups of sugar, three cups of flour and four eggs. Get the idea? So I made the batter for a 1234 Cake and baked it in a muffin tin to make cupcakes. Mom helped us with the oven part. But then we each had our own little cake to decorate—and eat, of course.

4. What's in a Hummingbird Cake?

Tess: This is a three-layer cake with cream-cheese frosting. It has pineapple, bananas and pecans in it—

but no hummingbirds. It's gooey-delicious! This cake gets gobbled up so fast, that some people call it the Nothing Left Cake. Did you know that hummingbirds eat very fast too? Thirteen licks a second! So maybe that's how this cake got its funny name.

5. What's the difference between Angel Food and Devil's Food cake?

Tess: That's easy. One of these cakes is fluffy, light and airy like angels. It's made with lots of egg whites. The other one is made with dark chocolate and is devilishly delicious. So I'm sure you can guess which one is which.

6. Do you know how cakes were invented?

Tess: Cakes have been around since ancient times. But in the beginning, they started out as bread sweetened with honey and nuts. People ate them at celebrations. A long time ago, cakes were rolled into a ball by hand and baked. So they were mostly round in those days. Now we have pans to make cakes in all shapes and sizes. The dictionary says that the word "cake" comes from the old Scandinavian word "kaka." I'm glad we call it cake!

7. How long have birthday cakes been around?

Tess: Birthday cakes started about two hundred years ago. At one time, people used to write "Many Happy Returns" on top of the cakes. The phrase "Happy Birthday" didn't start until the song "Happy Birthday to You" came out in 1910. I think we should write "Happy Cake Eating" on top of every single cake, don't you?

Pat Skene has no strange pets or weird habits like some of her characters do; however, she does have eleven rocking chairs and two outdoor swings. Could that be where she gets her wonderful sense of rhythm? Pat lives with her husband in Cobourg, Ontario.